THE POWER OF AWARENESS

NEVILLE GODDARD

adhyaya
BOOK'S HOUSE

Published by

ADHYAYA BOOKS HOUSE,

International Youth Club H-294, Plot 2A, First floor, Kehar Singh Estate, Saidulajab, Lane No.2 Saket, New Delhi - 110030

Ph : +91 72762 00890

E-mail : adhyaya.bks@gmail.com

Edition : 2021

ISBN : 9789394178038

Published by Adhyaya Books House LLP.

Neville Lancelot Goddard generally known simply as Neville, was an American author who wrote on the Bible, mysticism, and self-help.

Neville came to the United States to study drama at the age of seventeen. During his entertaining tour in England as a vaudeville dancer and stage actor, he developed a great interest in metaphysics. Hence, he gave up his entertainment job and devote fully to the study of metaphysics and spiritual matters. Neville gives the readers the necessary tools to understand and manifest what they desire in their lives.

According to Goddard, the stories of Esau and Jacob, sons of Issac, are a metaphor of the method by which men manifest their desires.

CONTENTS

Leave the mirror and change your face.

Leave the world alone and change your conceptions of yourself.

NEVILLE

CHAPTER I I AM

All things when they are admitted are made manifest by the light: for everything that is made manifest is light. Eph. 5:13.

The "light" is consciousness. Consciousness is one, manifesting in legions of forms or levels of consciousness. There is no one that is not all that is, for consciousness, though expressed in an infinite series of levels, is not divisional. There is no real separation or gap in consciousness. I AM cannot be divided. I may conceive myself to be a rich man, a poor man, a beggar man or a thief, but the center of my being remains the same regardless of the concept I hold of myself. At the center of manifestation there is only one I AM manifesting in legions of forms or concepts of itself and "I am that I am."

I AM is the self-definition of the absolute, the foundation on which everything rests. I AM is the first cause-substance. I AM is the self-definition of God.

I AM hath sent me unto you.

I AM THAT I AM.

Be still and know that I AM God.

I AM is a feeling of permanent awareness. The very center of conscious- ness is the feeling of I AM I may forget who I am, where I am, what I am but I cannot forget that I AM. The awareness of being remains, regardless of the degree of forgetfulness of who, where, and what I am.

I AM is that which, amid unnumbered forms is ever the same. This great discovery of cause reveals that, good or bad, man is actually the arbiter of his own fate, and that it is his concept of himself that determines the world in which he lives [and his concept of himself is his reactions to life]* In other words. If you are experiencing ill health, knowing the truth about cause, you cannot attribute the illness to anything other than to the particular arrangement of the basic cause-substance, an arrangement which [was produced by your reactions to life, and] is defined by your concept "I am unwell." This is why you are told "Let the weak man say, 'I am strong' " (Joel 3:10), for by his assumption, the cause-substance — I AM — is rearranged and must, therefore, manifest that which its rearrangement affirms. This principle governs every aspect of your life, be it social, financial, intellectual, or spiritual.

I AM is that reality to which, whatever happens, we must turn for an explanation of the phenomena of life. It is I AM's concept of itself that determines the form and scenery of its existence. Everything depends upon its attitude towards itself; that which it will not affirm as true of itself cannot awaken in its world. That is, your concept of yourself, such as "I am strong," "I am secure," "I am loved," determines the world in which you live. In other words, when you say, "I am a man, I am a father, I am an

American," you are not defining different I AMs; you are defining different concepts or arrangements of the one cause-substance — the one I AM. Even in the phenomena of nature, if the tree were articulate it would say, "I am a tree, an apple tree, a fruitful tree."

When you know that consciousness is the one and only reality-conceiving itself to be something good, bad, or indifferent, and becoming that which It conceived itself to be - you are free from the tyranny of second causes, free from the belief that there are causes outside of your own mind that can affect your life.

In the state of consciousness of the individual is found the explanation of the phenomena of life. If man's concept of himself were different, everything in his world would be different. His concept of himself being what it is, everything in his world must be as it is.

Thus it is abundantly clear that there is only one I AM and you are that I AM. And while I AM is infinite, you, by your concept of yourself, are dis- playing only a limited aspect of the infinite I AM.

Build thee more stately mansions, O my soul.

As the swift seasons roll!

Leave thy low-vaulted past!

Let each new temple, nobler than the last.

Shut thee from heaven with a dome more vast

Till thou at length art free,

Leaving thine outgrown shell by life's unresting sea!

CHAPTER II
CONCIOUSNESS

It is only by a change of consciousness, by actually changing your concept of yourself, that you can "build more stately mansions" — the manifestations of higher and higher concepts. (By manifesting is meant experiencing the results of these concepts in your world.) It is of vital importance to understand clearly just what consciousness is.

The reason lies in the fact that consciousness is the one and only reality, it is the first and only cause -sub stance of the phenomena of life. Nothing has existence for man save through the consciousness he has of it. Therefore, it is to consciousness you must turn, for it is the only foundation on which the phenomena of life can be explained.

If we accept the idea of a first cause, it would follow that the evolution of that cause could never result in anything foreign to itself. That is, if the first cause-substance is light, all its evolutions, fruits, and manifestations would remain light. The first cause-substance being consciousness, all its evolutions, fruits, and phenomena must remain consciousness. All that could be observed would be a higher or lower form or variation of the same thing. In other words, if your consciousness is the only reality, it must also be the only substance. Consequently, what appears to you as circumstances, conditions, and even material objects are really only the products of your own consciousness. Nature, then, as a thing or a complex of things external to your mind, must be rejected. You and your environment cannot be regarded as existing separately. You and your world are one.

Therefore, you must turn from the objective appearance of things to the subjective center of things, your consciousness, if you truly desire to know the cause of the phenomena of life, and how to use this knowledge to realize your fondest dreams. In the midst of the apparent contradictions, antagonisms, and contrasts of your life, there is only one principle at work, only your consciousness operating. Difference does not consist in variety of substance, but in variety of arrangement of the same cause-substance, your consciousness.

The world moves with motiveless necessity. By this is meant that it has no motive of its own, but is under the necessity of manifesting your concept, the arrangement of your mind, and your mind is always arranged in the image of all you believe and consent to as true. The rich man, poor man, beggar man or thief are not different minds, but different arrangements of the same mind, in the same sense that a piece of steel when magnetized differs not in substance from its demagnetized state but in the arrangement and order of its molecules. A single electron revolving in a specified orbit constitutes the unit of magnetism. When a piece of steel or anything else is demagnetized, the revolving electrons have not stopped. Therefore, the magnetism has not gone out of existence. There is only a rearrangement of the particles, so that they produce no outside or perceptible effect. When particles are arranged at random, mixed up in all directions, the substance is said to be demagnetized-but when particles are marshalled in ranks so that a number of them face in one direction, the substance is a magnet. Magnetism is not generated; it is displayed. Health, wealth, beauty, and genius are not created; they are only manifested by the arrangement of your mind-that is, by your concept of yourself [and your concept of yourself is all that you accept and consent to as true. What you consent to can only be discovered by an uncritical observation of your reactions to life. Your reactions reveal where you live psychologically; and where you live psychologically, determines how you live here in the outer visible world]. The importance of this in your daily life should be immediately apparent.

The basic nature of the primal cause is consciousness. Therefore, the ultimate substance of all things is consciousness.

CHAPTER III POWER OF ASSUMPTION

Man's chief delusion is his conviction that there are causes other than his own state of consciousness. All that befalls a man — all that is done by him — all that comes from him — happens as a result of his state of consciousness. A man's consciousness is all that he thinks and desires and loves, all that he believes is true and consents to. That is why a change of consciousness is necessary before you can change your outer world. Rain falls as a result of a change in the temperature in the higher regions of the atmosphere, so, in like manner, a change of circumstance happens as a result of a change in your state of consciousness.

Be ye transformed by the renewing of your mind.

To be transformed, the whole basis of your thoughts must change. But your thoughts cannot change unless you have new ideas, for you think from your ideas. All transformation begins with an intense, burning desire to be transformed. The first step in the "renewing of the mind" is desire. You must want to be different [and intend to be] before you can begin to change yourself. Then you must make your future dream a present fact. You do this by assuming the feeling of your wish fulfilled. By desiring to be other than what you are, you can create an ideal of the person you want to be and assume that you are already that person. If this assumption is persisted in until it becomes your dominant feeling, the attainment of your ideal is inevitable. The ideal you hope to achieve is always ready for an incarnation, but unless you yourself offer it human parentage, it is incapable of birth. Therefore, your attitude should be one in which - having desired to express a higher state-you alone accept the task of incarnating this new and greater value of yourself.

In giving birth to your ideal you must bear in mind that the methods of mental and spiritual knowledge are entirely different. This is a point that IS truly understood by probably not more than one person in a million. You know a thing mentally by looking at it from the outside, by comparing it with other things, by analyzing it and defining if [by thinking of it:] whereas you can know a thing spiritually only by becoming it, [only by thinking from it]. You must be the thing itself and not merely talk about it or look at it. You must be like the moth in search of his idol, the flame, who spurred with true desire, plunging at once into the sacred fire, folded his wings within, till he became one colour and one substance with the flame. He only knew the flame who in it burned, and only he could tell who ne'er to tell returned.

Just as the moth in his desire to know the flame was willing to destroy himself, so must you in becoming a new person be willing to die to your present self.

You must be conscious of being healthy if you are to know what health is. You must be conscious of being secure if you are to know what security is. Therefore, to incarnate a new and greater value of yourself, you must assume that you already are what you want to be and then live by faith in this assumption — which is not yet incarnate in the body of your life — in confidence that this new value or state of consciousness will become in- carnated through your absolute fidelity to the assumption that you are that which you desire to be. This is what wholeness means, what integrity means. They mean. submission of the whole self to the feeling of the wish fulfilled in certainty that that new state of consciousness is the renewing of mind which transforms. There is no order in Nature corresponding to this willing submission of the self to the ideal beyond the self. Therefore, it is the height of folly to expect the incarnation of a new and greater concept of self to come about by natural evolutionary process. That which requires a state of consciousness to produce its effect obviously cannot be effected without such a state of consciousness, and in your ability to assume the feeling of a greater life, to assume a new concept of yourself, you possess what the rest of Nature does not possess — Imagination — the instrument by which you create your world.

Your imagination is the instrument, the means, whereby your redemption from slavery, sickness, and poverty is effected. If you refuse to assume the responsibility of the incarnation of a new and higher concept of yourself, then you reject the means, the only means, whereby your redemption — that is, the attainment of your ideal — can be effected.

Imagination is the only redemptive power in the universe. However, your nature is such that it is optional to you whether you remain in your present concept of yourself (a hungry being longing for freedom, health, and security) or choose to become the instrument of your own redemption, imagining yourself as that which you want to be, and thereby satisfying your hunger and redeeming yourself.

O be strong then, and brave,

pure, patient and true;

The work that is yours let no

other hand do.

For the strength

From the fountain within you

— the Kingdom of Heaven.

CHAPTER IV DESIRE

The changes which take place in your life as a result of your changed concept of yourself always appear to the unenlightened to be the result, not of a change of your consciousness, but of chance, outer cause, or coincidence. However, the only fate governing your life is the fate determ- ined by your own concepts, your own assumptions; for an assumption, though false, if persisted in will harden into fact. The ideal you seek and hope to attain will not manifest itself, will not be realized by you, until you have imagined that you are already that ideal. There is no escape for you except by a radical psychological transformation of yourself, except by your assumption of the feeling of your wish fulfilled. Therefore, make results or accomplishments the crucial test of your ability to use your imagination.

Everything depends on your attitude towards yourself. That which you will not affirm as true of yourself can never he realized by you, for that attitude alone is the necessary condition by which you realize your goal.

All transformation is based upon suggestion, and this can work only where you lay yourself completely open to an influence. You must abandon yourself to your ideal as a woman abandons herself to love, for complete abandonment of self to it is the way to union with your ideal. You must assume the feeling of the wish fulfilled until your assumption has all the sensory vividness of reality. You must imagine that you are already experiencing what you desire. That is, you must assume the feeling of the fulfillment of your desire until you are possessed by it and this feeling crowds all other ideas out of your consciousness.

The man who is not prepared for the conscious plunge into the assumption of the wish fulfilled in the faith that it is the only way to the realization of his dream is not yet ready to live consciously by the law of assumption, although there is no doubt that he does live by the law of assumption unconsciously. But for you who accept this principle and are ready to live by consciously assuming that your wish is already fulfilled, the adventure of life begins. To reach a higher level of being, you must assume a higher concept of yourself.

If you will not imagine yourself as other than what you are, then you remain as you are, for if ye believe not that I am He, ye shall die in your sins.

If you do not believe that you are He (the person you want to be), then you remain as you are. Through the faithful systematic cultivation of the feeling of the wish fulfilled, desire becomes the promise of its own fulfillment. The assumption of the feeling of the wish fulfilled makes the future dream a present fact.

CHAPTER V THE TRUTH THAT SETS YOU FREE

The drama of life is a psychological one in which all the conditions, circumstances, and events of your life are brought to pass by your assumptions.

Since your life is determined by your assumptions, you are forced to recognize the fact that you are either a slave to your assumptions or their master. To become the master of your assumptions is the key to undreamed-of freedom and happiness. You can attain this mastery by deliberate conscious control of your imagination. You determine your assumptions in this way: Form a mental image, a picture of the state desired, of the person you want to be. Concentrate your attention upon the feeling that you are already that person. First, visualize the picture in your consciousness. Then feel yourself to be in that state as though it actually formed your surrounding world. By your imagination that which was a mere mental image is changed into a seemingly solid reality.

The great secret is a controlled imagination and a well-sustained attention firmly and repeatedly focused on the object to be accomplished. It cannot be emphasized too much that, by creating an ideal within your mental sphere, by assuming that you are already that ideal, *you identify yourself with it and thereby transform yourself into its image, [thinking from the ideal instead of thinking of the ideal. Every state is already there as "mere possibilities" as long as we think of them, but as overpoweringly real when we think from them]*. This was called by the ancient teachers "Subjection to the will of God" or "Resting in the

Lord," and the only true test of "Resting in the Lord" is that all who do rest are inevitably transformed into the image of that in which they rest [thinking from the wish fulfilled]. You become according to your resigned will, and your resigned will is your concept of yourself and all that you consent to and accept as true. You, assuming the feeling of your wish fulfilled and continuing therein, take upon yourself the results of that state; not assuming the feeling of your wish fulfilled, you are ever free of the results.

When you understand the redemptive function of imagination, you hold in your hands the key to the solution of all your problems. Every phase of your life is made by the exercise of your imagination. Determined imagination alone is the means of your progress, of the fulfilling of your dreams. It is the beginning and end of all creating. The great secret is a controlled imagination and a well-sustained attention firmly and repeatedly focused on the feeling of the wish fulfilled until it fills the mind and crowds all other ideas out of consciousness. What greater gifts could be given you than to be told the Truth that will set you free? The Truth that sets you free is that you can experience in imagination what you desire to experience in reality, and by maintaining this experience in imagination, your desire will become an actuality.

You are limited only by your uncontrolled imagination and lack of attention to the feeling of your wish fulfilled. When the imagination is not controlled and the attention not steadied on the feeling of the wish fulfilled, then no amount of prayer or piety or invocation will produce the desired effect. When you can call up at will whatsoever image you please, when the forms of your imagination are as vivid to you as the forms of nature, you are master of your fate. *[You must stop spending your thoughts, your time and your money. Everything in life must*

be an investment.]

Visions of beauty and splendor,

Forms of a long-lost race,

Sounds and faces and voices.

From the fourth dimension of space —

And on through the universe boundless,

Our thoughts go lightning

shod —

Some call it imagination,

And other call it God

◊ Neville follows this with the date April 12, [19]53. In Awakened Imagination (1954) he would write, "On the morning of April 12, 1953, my wife was awakened by the sound of a great voice of authority speaking within her and saying, 'You must stop spending your thoughts, time, and money. Everything in life must be an investment.' To spend is to waste, to squander, to layout without return. To invest is to lay out for a purpose from which a profit is expected. This revelation of my wife is about the importance of the moment. It is about the transformation of the moment. . . . It is only what is done now that counts. Whenever we assume the feeling of being what we want to be, we are investing." (ch. 5) — Ed.

CHAPTER VI ATTENTION

A double-minded man is unstable in all his ways. James 1:8.

Attention is forceful in proportion to the narrowness of its focus, that is, when it is obsessed with a single idea or sensation. It is steadied and powerfully focused only by such an adjustment of the mind as permits you to see one thing only, for you steady the attention and increase its power by confining it. The desire which realizes itself is always a desire upon which attention is exclusively concentrated, for an idea is endowed with power only in proportion, to the degree of attention fixed on it. Concentrated observation is the attentive attitude directed [from]* some specific end. The attentive attitude involves selection, for when you pay attention, it signifies that you have decided to focus your attention on one object or state rather than on another.

Therefore, when you know what you want, you must deliberately focus your attention on the feeling of your wish fulfilled until that feeling fills the mind and crowds all other ideas out of consciousness.

The power of attention is the measure of your inner force. Concentrated observation of one thing shuts out other things and causes them to disappear. The great secret of success is to focus the attention on the feeling of the wish fulfilled without permitting any distraction. All progress depends upon an increase of attention. The ideas which impel you to action are those which dominate the consciousness, those which possess the attention. [The idea which excludes all others from the field of attention discharges in action.]

---

*Neville substitutes from for towards, the reading in the original. —Ed.

This one thing I do, forgetting those things that are behind, I press toward the mark.

This means you, this one thing you can do, "forgetting those things that are behind." You can press toward the mark of filling your mind with the feeling of the wish fulfilled.

To the unenlightened man this will seem to be all fantasy, yet all progress comes from those who do not take the accepted view, nor accept the world as it is. As was stated heretofore, if you can imagine what you please, and if the forms of your thought are as vivid as the forms of nature, you are by virtue of the power of your imagination master of your fate.

Your imagination is you yourself, and the world as your imagination sees it is the real world.

When you set out to master the movements of attention, which must be done if you would successfully alter the course of observed events, it is then you realize how little control you exercise over your imagination and how much it is dominated by sensory impressions and by a drifting on the tides of idle moods.

To aid in mastering the control of your attention, practice this exercise: Night after night, just before you drift off to sleep, strive to hold your attention on the activities of the day in reverse order. Focus your attention on the last thing you did, that is, getting in to bed, and then move it backward in time over the events until you reach the first event of the day, getting out of bed. This is no easy exercise, but just as specific exercises greatly help in developing specific muscles, this will greatly help in developing the "muscle" of your attention. Your attention must be developed, controlled, and concentrated in order to change your concept of yourself successfully and thereby change your future. Imagination is able to do anything, but only according to the internal direction of your attention. If you persist night after night, sooner or later you will awaken in yourself a centre of power and become conscious of your greater self, the real you. Attention is developed by repeated exercise or habit. Through habit an action becomes easier, and so in course of time gives rise to a facility or faculty, which can then be put to higher uses.

When you attain control of the internal direction of your attention, you will no longer stand in shallow water but will launch out into the deep of life. You will walk in the assumption of the wish fulfilled as on a foundation more solid even than earth.

CHAPTER VII ATTITUDE

Experiments recently conducted by Merle Lawrence (Princeton) and Adelbert Ames (Dartmouth) in the latter's psychology laboratory at Hanover, N.H., prove that what you see when you look at something depends not so much on what is there as on the assumption you make when you look. Since what we believe to be the "real" physical world is actually only an "assumptive" world, it is not surprising that these experiments prove that what appears to be solid reality is actually the result of "expectations" or "assumptions." Your assumptions determine not only what you see but also what you do, for they govern all your conscious and subconscious movements towards the fulfillment of themselves. Over a century ago this truth was stated by Emerson as follows:

As the world was plastic and fluid in the hands of God, so it is ever to so much of his attributes as we bring to it. To ignorance and sin, it is flint. They adapt themselves to it as they may, but in proportion as a man has anything in him divine, the firmament flows before him and takes his signet and form.

Your assumption is the hand of God moulding the firmament into the image of that which you assume. The assumption of the wish fulfilled is the high tide which lifts you easily off the bar of the senses where you have so long lain stranded. It lifts the mind into prophecy in the full right sense of the word; and if you have that controlled imagination and absorbed attention which it is possible to attain, you may be sure that all your assumption implies will come to pass.

When William Blake wrote,

'What seems to be, is, to those to whom it seems to be' he was only repeating the eternal truth, there is nothing unclean of itself: but to him that esteemeth anything to be unclean, to him it is unclean. Rom. 14:14.

Because there is nothing unclean of itself {or clean of itself), you should assume the best and think only of that which is lovely and of good report. It is not superior insight but ignorance of this law of assumption if you read into the greatness of men some littleness with which you may be familiar— or into some situation or circumstance an unfavorable conviction. Your particular relationship to another influences your assumption with respect to that other and makes you see in him that which you do see. If you can change your opinion of another, then what you now believe of him cannot be absolutely true but is only relatively true. The following is an actual case history illustrating how the law of assumption works:

One day a costume designer described to me her difficulties in working with a prominent theatrical producer. She was convinced that he unjustly criticized and rejected her best work and that often he was deliberately rude and unfair to her. Upon hearing her story, I explained that if she found the other rude and unfair, it was a sure sign that she, herself, was wanting and that it was not the producer, but herself that was in need of a new attitude. I told her that the power of this law of assumption and its practical application could be discovered only through experience, and that only by assuming that the situation was already what she wanted it to be could she prove that she could bring about the change desired. Her employer was merely bearing witness, telling her by his behavior what her concept of him was. I suggested that it was quite probable that she was carrying on conversations with him in her mind which were filled with criticism and recriminations. There was no doubt but that she was mentally arguing with the producer, for others only echo that which we whisper to them in secret. I asked her if it was not true that she talked to him mentally, and, if so, what those conversations were like. She confessed that every morning on her way to the theatre she told him just what she thought of him in a way she would never have dared address him in person. The intensity and force of her mental arguments with him automatically established his behavior towards her. She began to realize that all of us carry on mental conversations, but, unfortunately, on most occasions these conversations are argumentative . . . that we have only to observe the passerby on the street to prove this assertion . . . that so many people are mentally engrossed in conversation and few appear to be happy about it, but the very intensity of their feeling must lead them quickly to the unpleasant incident they themselves have mentally created and therefore must now encounter. When she realized what she had been doing, she agreed to change her attitude and to live this law faithfully by assuming that her job was highly satisfactory and her relationship with the producer was a very happy one. To do this she agreed that before going to sleep at night, on her way to work, and at other intervals during the day she would imagine that he had congratulated her on her fine designs and that she, in turn, had thanked him for his praise and kindness. To her great delight she soon discovered for herself that her own attitude was the cause of all that befell her.

The behavior of her employer miraculously reversed itself. His attitude, echoing, as it had always done, that which she had assumed, now reflected her changed concept of him. What she did was by the power of her imagination. Her persistent assumption influenced his behavior and determined his attitude toward her. With the passport of desire on the wings of a controlled imagination she traveled into the future of her own predetermined experience. Thus we see it is not facts, but that which we create in our imagination, which shapes our lives, for most of the conflicts of the day are due to the want of a little imagination to cast the beam out of our own eye. It is the exact and literal-minded who live in a fictitious world. As this designer, by her controlled imagination, started the subtle change in her employer's mind, so can we, by the control of our own imagination and wisely directed feeling, solve our problems.

By the intensity of her imagination and feeling, the designer cast a kind of enchantment on her producer's mind and caused him to think that his generous praise originated with him. Often our most elaborate and original thoughts are determined by another.

We should never be certain that it was not some woman treading in the wine-press who began that subtle change in men's mind, or that the passion did not begin in the mind of some shepherd boy, lighting up his eyes for a moment before it ran upon its way.

William Butler Yeats

CHAPTER VIII
RENUNCIATION

There is no coal of character so dead that it will not glow and flame if but slightly turned.

Resist not evil.

Whosoever shall smite thee on thy right cheek, turn to him the other also.

There is a great difference between resisting evil and renouncing it. When you resist evil, you give it your attention, you continue to make it real. When you renounce evil, you take your attention from it and give your attention to what you want. Now is the time to control your imagination and give beauty for ashes, joy for mourning, praise for the spirit of heaviness, that they might be called trees of righteousness, the planting of the Lord that He might be glorified.

You give beauty for ashes when you concentrate your attention on things as you would like them to be rather than on things as they are. You give joy for mourning when you maintain a joyous attitude regardless of unfavorable circumstances. You give praise for the spirit of heaviness when you maintain a confident attitude instead of succumbing to despondency. In this quotation the Bible uses the word tree as a synonym for man. You become a tree of righteousness when the above mental states are a permanent part of your consciousness. You are a planting of the Lord when all your thoughts are true thoughts. He is I AM as described in Chapter One. I AM is glorified when your highest concept of yourself is manifested.

When you have discovered your own controlled imagination to be your saviour, your attitude will be completely altered without any diminution of religious feeling, and you will say of your controlled imagination.

Behold this vine. I found it a wild tree, whose wanton strength had swollen into irregular twigs. But I pruned the plant and it grew temperate in its vain expense of useless leaves, and knotted as you see into these clean full clusters to repay the hand that wisely wounded it.

By vine is meant your imagination, which, in its uncontrolled state, expends its energy in useless or destructive thoughts and feelings. But you, just as the vine is pruned by cutting away its useless branches and roots, prune your imagination by withdrawing your attention from all unlovely and destructive ideas and concentrating on the ideal you wish to attain. The happier, more noble life you will experience will be the result of wisely pruning your own imagination. Yes, be pruned of all unlovely thoughts and feelings that you may think truly, and thy thoughts shall the world's famine feed; Speak truly, and each word of thine shall be a fruitful seed; Live truly, and thy life shall be a great and noble creed.

CHAPTER IX PREPARING YOUR PLACE

And all mine are thine, and thine are mine. John 17:10.

Thrust in thy sickle, and reap; for the time is come for thee to reap; for the harvest of the earth is ripe. Rev. 14:15.

All is yours. Do not go seeking for that which you are. Appropriate it, claim it, assume it. Everything depends upon your concept of yourself.

That which you do not claim as true of yourself cannot be realized by you. The promise is:

Whosoever hath, to him it shall be given, and he shall have more abundance; but whosoever hath not, from him shall be taken away even that which he seemeth to have.

Hold fast, in your imagination, to all that is lovely and of good report, for the lovely and the good are essential in your life if it is to be worthwhile. Assume it. You do this by imagining that you already are what you want to be — and already have what you want to have.

As a man thinketh in his heart so is he.

Be still and know that you are that which you desire to be, and you will never have to search for it.

In spite of your appearance of freedom of action, you obey, as everything else does, the law of assumption. Whatever you may think of the question of free will, the truth is your experiences throughout your life are determined by your assumptions — whether conscious or unconscious. An as- sumption builds a bridge of incidents that lead inevitably to the fulfillment of itself.

Man believes the future to be the natural development of the past. But the law of assumption clearly shows that this is not the case. Your assumption places you psychologically where you are not physically; then your senses pull you back from where you were psychologically to where you are physically. It is these psychological forward motions that produce your physical forward motions in time. Precognition permeates all the scriptures of the world.

In my Father's house are many mansions; If it were not so, I would have told you. I go to prepare a place for you. And if I go and prepare a place for you, I will come again and receive you unto myself: that where I am, there ye may be also. . . . And now I have told you before it came to pass, that, when it is come to pass, ye might believe. John 14:2, 3, 29.

The "I" in this quotation is your imagination which goes into the future, into one of the many mansions. Mansion is the state desired . . . telling of an event before it occurs physically is simply feeling yourself into the state desired until it has the tone of reality. You go and prepare a place for yourself by imagining yourself into the feeling of your wish fulfilled. Then, you speed from this state of the wish fulfilled — where you have not been physically — back to where you were physically a moment ago. Then, with an irresistible forward movement, you move forward across a series of events to the physical realization of your wish, that where you have been in imagination, there you will be in the flesh also.

Unto the place from whence the rivers come, thither they return again. Eccles. 1:7.

CHAPTER X CREATION

I am God, declaring the end from the beginning, and from ancient times things that are not yet done. Isaiah 46:9, 10.

Creation is finished. Creativeness is only a deeper receptiveness, for the entire contents of all time and all space, while experienced in a time sequence, actually coexist in an infinite and eternal now. In other words, all that you ever have been or ever will be — in fact, all that mankind ever was or ever will be — exists now. This is what is meant by creation, and the statement that creation is finished means nothing is ever to be created, it is only to be manifested. What is called creativeness is only becoming aware of what already is. You simply become aware of increasing portions of that which already exists. The fact that you can never be anything that you are not already or experience anything not already existing explains the experience of having an acute feeling of having heard before what is being said, or having met before the person being met for the first time, or having seen before a place or thing being seen for the first time.

The whole of creation exists in you, and it is your destiny to become increasingly aware of its infinite wonders and to experience ever greater and grander portions of it.

If creation is finished, and all events are taking place now, the question that springs naturally to the mind is "what determines your time track?" That is, what determines the events which you encounter? And the answer is your concept of yourself . Concepts determine the route that attention follows. Here is a good test to prove this fact. Assume the feeling of your wish fulfilled and observe the route that your attention follows.

You will observe that as long as you remain faithful to your assumption, so long will your attention be confronted with images clearly related to that assumption. For example; if you assume that you have a wonderful business, you will notice how in your imagination your attention is focused on incident after incident relating to that assumption. Friends congratulate you, tell you how lucky you are.

Others are envious and critical. From there your attention goes to larger offices, bigger bank balances, and many other similarly related events.

Persistence in this assumption will result in *actually experiencing in fact that which you assumed.*

The same is true regarding any concept. If your concept of yourself is that you are a failure, you would encounter in your imagination a whole series of incidents in conformance to that concept.

Thus it is clearly seen how you, by your concept of yourself, determine your present, that is, the particular portion of creation which you now ex- perience, and your future, that is, the particular portion of creation which you will experience.

CHAPTER XI INTERFERENCE

You ARE free to choose the concept you will accept of yourself. Therefore, you possess the power of intervention, the power which enables you to alter the course of your future. The process of rising from your present concept to a higher concept of yourself is the means of all true progress. The higher concept is waiting for you to incarnate it in the world of experience.

Now unto Him that is able to do exceeding abundantly above all that we ask or think, according to the power that worketh in us, unto him be glory. Eph. 3:20.

Him, that is able to do more than you can ask or think, is your imagination, and the power that worketh in us is your attention. Understanding imagination to be HIM that is able to do all that you ask, and attention to be the power by which you create your world, you can now build your ideal world. Imagine yourself to be the ideal you dream of and desire. Remain attentive to this imagined state, and as fast as you completely feel that you are already this ideal it will manifest itself as reality in your world.

He was in the world, and the world was made by him and the world knew him not.

The mystery hid from the ages; Christ in you, the hope of glory.

The "He," in the first of these quotations, is your imagination. As previously explained, there is only one substance. This substance is consciousness. It is your imagination which forms this substance into concepts, which concepts are then manifested as conditions, circumstances, and physical objects. Thus imagination made your world. This supreme truth with but few exceptions man is not conscious of.

The mystery, Christ in you, referred to in the second quotation, is your imagination, by which your world is molded. The hope of glory is your awareness of the ability to rise perpetually to higher levels.

Christ is not to be found in history nor in external forms. You find Christ only when you become aware of the fact that your imagination is the only redemptive power. When this is discovered, the "towers of dogma will have heard the trumpets of Truth, and, like the walls of Jericho, crumble to dust."

CHAPTER XII SUBJECTIVE CONTROL

Your imagination is able to do all that you ask in proportion to the degree of your attention. All progress, all fulfillment of desire, depend upon the control and concentration of your attention. Attention may be either attracted from without or directed from within. Attention is attracted from without when you are consciously occupied with the external impressions of the immediate present. The very lines of this page are attracting your attention from without. Your attention is directed from within when you deliberately choose what you will be preoccupied with mentally. It is obvious that in the objective world your attention is not only attracted by but is constantly directed to external impressions. But, your control in the subjective state is almost non-existent, for in this state attention is usually the servant and not the master — the passenger and not the navigator — of your world.

There is an enormous difference between attention directed objectively and attention directed subjectively, and the capacity to change your future depends on the latter. When you are able to control the movements of your attention in the subjective world, you can modify or alter your life as you please. But this control cannot be achieved if you allow your attention to be attracted constantly from without. Each day, set yourself the task of deliberately withdrawing your attention from the objective world and of focusing it subjectively. In other words, concentrate on those thoughts or moods which you deliberately determine. Then those things that now restrict you will fade and drop away. The day you achieve control of the movements of your attention in the subjective world, you are mas- ter of your fate.

You will no longer accept the dominance of outside conditions or circumstances. You will not accept life on the basis of the world without. Having achieved control of the movements of your attention, and having discovered the mystery hid from the ages, that Christ in you is your imagination, you will assert the supremacy of imagination and put all things in subjection to it.

CHAPTER XIII ACCEPTANCE

Man's Perceptions are not bounded by organs of Perception: he perceives more than sense (though ever so acute) can discover.

However much you seem to be living in a material world, you are actually living in a world of imagination. The outer, physical events of life are the fruit of forgotten blossom-times — results of previous and usually forgotten states of consciousness. They are the ends running true to ofttimes forgotten imaginative origins.

Whenever you become completely absorbed in an emotional state, you are at that moment assuming the feeling of the state fulfilled. If persisted in, whatsoever you are intensely emotional about you will experience in your world. These periods of absorption, of concentrated attention, are the beginnings of the things you harvest. It is in such moments that you are exercising your creative power — the only creative power there is. At the end of these periods, or moments of absorption, you speed from these imaginative states (where you have not been physically) to where you were physically an instant ago. In these periods the imagined state is so real that when you return to the objective world and find that it is not the same as the imagined state, it is an actual shock. You have seen something in imagination with such vividness that you now wonder whether the evidence of your senses can now be believed, and like Keats you ask,

was it a vision or a waking dream?

Fled is that music . . . Do I wake or sleep?

This shock reverses your time sense. By this is meant that instead of your experience resulting from your past, it now becomes the result of being in imagination where you have not yet been physically. In effect, this moves you across a bridge of incident to the physical realization of your imagined state. The man who at will can assume whatever state he pleases has found the keys to the Kingdom of Heaven. The keys are desire, imagination, and a steadily focused attention on the feeling of the wish fulfilled. To such a man any undesirable objective fact is no longer a reality and the ardent wish no longer a dream.

Prove me now herewith, saith the Lord of hosts, if I will not open you the windows of heaven, and pour you out a blessing, that there shall not be room enough to receive it. Malachi 3:10.

The windows of heaven may not be opened and the treasures seized by a strong will, but they open of themselves and present their treasures as a free gift — a gift that comes when absorption reaches such a degree that it results in a feeling of complete acceptance. The passage from your present state to the feeling of your wish fulfilled is not across a gap.

There is continuity between the so-called real and unreal. To cross from one state to the other, you simply extend your feelers, trust your touch, and enter fully into the spirit of what you are doing.

Not by might nor by power but by my spirit, saith the Lord of hosts.

Assume the spirit, the feeling of the wish fulfilled, and you will have opened the windows to receive the blessing. To assume a state is to get into the spirit of it. Your triumphs will be a surprise only to those who did not know your hidden passage from the state of longing to the assumption of the wish fulfilled.

The Lord of hosts will not respond to your wish until you have assumed the feeling of already being what you want to be, for acceptance is the channel of His action. Acceptance is the Lord of hosts in action.

CHAPTER XIII ACCEPTANCE

Man's Perceptions are not bounded by organs of Perception: he perceives more than sense (though ever so acute) can discover.

However much you seem to be living in a material world, you are actually living in a world of imagination. The outer, physical events of life are the fruit of forgotten blossom-times — results of previous and usually forgotten states of consciousness. They are the ends running true to ofttimes forgotten imaginative origins.

Whenever you become completely absorbed in an emotional state, you are at that moment assuming the feeling of the state fulfilled. If persisted in, whatsoever you are intensely emotional about you will experience in your world. These periods of absorption, of concentrated attention, are the beginnings of the things you harvest. It is in such moments that you are exercising your creative power — the only creative power there is. At the end of these periods, or moments of absorption, you speed from these imaginative states (where you have not been physically) to where you were physically an instant ago. In these periods the imagined state is so real that when you return to the objective world and find that it is not the same as the imagined state, it is an actual shock. You have seen something in imagination with such vividness that you now wonder whether the evidence of your senses can now be believed, and like Keats you ask,

was it a vision or a waking dream?

Fled is that music . . . Do I wake or sleep?

This shock reverses your time sense. By this is meant that instead of your experience resulting from your past, it now becomes the result of being in imagination where you have not yet been physically. In effect, this moves you across a bridge of incident to the physical realization of your imagined state. The man who at will can assume whatever state he pleases has found the keys to the Kingdom of Heaven. The keys are desire, imagination, and a steadily focused attention on the feeling of the wish fulfilled. To such a man any undesirable objective fact is no longer a reality and the ardent wish no longer a dream.

Prove me now herewith, saith the Lord of hosts, if I will not open you the windows of heaven, and pour you out a blessing, that there shall not be room enough to receive it. Malachi 3:10.

The windows of heaven may not be opened and the treasures seized by a strong will, but they open of themselves and present their treasures as a free gift — a gift that comes when absorption reaches such a degree that it results in a feeling of complete acceptance. The passage from your present state to the feeling of your wish fulfilled is not across a gap.

There is continuity between the so-called real and unreal. To cross from one state to the other, you simply extend your feelers, trust your touch, and enter fully into the spirit of what you are doing.

Not by might nor by power but by my spirit, saith the Lord of hosts.

Assume the spirit, the feeling of the wish fulfilled, and you will have opened the windows to receive the blessing. To assume a state is to get into the spirit of it. Your triumphs will be a surprise only to those who did not know your hidden passage from the state of longing to the assumption of the wish fulfilled.

The Lord of hosts will not respond to your wish until you have assumed the feeling of already being what you want to be, for acceptance is the channel of His action. Acceptance is the Lord of hosts in action.

CHAPTER XIV THE EFFORTLESS WAY

The principle of "Least Action" governs everything in physics from the path of a planet to the path of a pulse of light. Least Action is the minimum of energy, multiplied by the minimum of time. Therefore, in moving from your present state to the state desired, you must use the minimum of energy and take the shortest possible time. Your journey from one state of consciousness to another is a psychological one, so, to make the journey, you must employ the psychological equivalent of "Least Action," and the psychological equivalent is mere assumption.

The day you fully realize the power of assumption, you discover that it works in complete conformity with this principle. It works by means of attention, minus effort. Thus, with least action through an assumption you hurry without haste and reach your goal without effort.

Because creation is finished, what you desire already exists. It is excluded from view because you can see only the contents of your own consciousness. It is the function of an assumption to call back the excluded view and restore full vision. It is not the world but your assumptions that change. An assumption brings the invisible into sight. It is nothing more nor less than seeing with the eye of God, i.e., imagination.

For the Lord seeth not as a man seeth, for man looketh on the outward appearance, but the Lord looketh on the heart.

The heart is the primary organ of sense, hence the first cause of experience. When you look "on the heart" you are looking at your assumptions: assumptions determine your experience. Watch your assumption with all diligence for out of it are the issues of life. Assumptions have the power of objective realization. Every event in the visible world is the result of an assumption or idea in the unseen world.

The present moment is all-important, for it is only in the present moment that our assumptions can be controlled. The future must become the present in your mind if you would wisely operate the law of assumption. The future becomes the present when you imagine that you already are what you will be when your assumption is fulfilled. Be still (least action) and know that you are that which you desire to be. The end of longing should be Being. Translate your dream into Being. Perpetual construction of future states without the consciousness of already being them, that is, picturing your desire without actually assuming the feeling of the wish fulfilled, is the fallacy and mirage of mankind.

It is simply futile day-dreaming.

CHAPTER XV THE CROWN OF THE MYSTERIES

The assumption of the wish fulfilled is the ship that carries you over the unknown seas to the fulfillment of your dream. The assumption is everything; realization is subconscious and effortless.

Assume a virtue if you have it not.

Act on the assumption that you already possess that which you sought.

Blessed is she that believed; for there shall be a performance of those things which were told her from the Lord.

As the Immaculate Conception* is the foundation of the Christian mysteries, so the Assumption** of is their crown. Psychologically the Immaculate Conception means the birth of an idea in your own consciousness unaided by another. For instance when you have a specific wish or hunger or longing, it is an immaculate conception in the sense that no physical person or thing plants it in your mind. It is self-conceived. Every man is the Mary of the Immaculate Conception and birth to his idea must give.*** The Assumption is the crown of the mysteries because it is the highest use of consciousness. When in imagination you assume the feeling of the wish fulfilled, you are mentally lifted up to a higher level. When, through your persistence, this assumption becomes actual fact, you automatically find yourself on

---

* Mary's birth without Original Sin. However, Neville seems to have in mind the Virgin Birth of Jesus. - Ed.

** The taking up of the body (usually, the body of Mary) into heaven. - Ed

.*** Stylistic inversion deriving from quotation not cited - and must give birth to his idea." - Ed.

a higher level (that is, you have achieved your desire) in your objective world. Your assumption guides all your conscious and subconscious movements towards its suggested end so inevitably that it actually dictates the events.

The drama of life is a psychological one and the whole of it is written and produced by your assumptions.

Learn the art of assumption, for only in this way can you create your own happiness.

CHAPTER XVI PERSONAL IMPOTENCE

Self surrender is essential, and by that is meant 'the confession of personal impotence.

I can of mine own self do nothing.

Since creation is finished, it is impossible to force anything into being. The example of magnetism previously given is a good illustration. You cannot make magnetism; it can only be displayed. You cannot make the law of magnetism. If you want to build a magnet, you can do so only by conforming to the law of magnetism. In other words, you surrender yourself, or yield to the law. In like manner, when you use the faculty of assumption, you are conforming to a law just as real as the law governing magnetism. You can neither create nor change the law of assumption. It is in this respect that you are impotent. You can only yield or conform, and since all of your experiences are the result of your assumptions (consciously or unconsciously) the value of consciously using the power of assumption surely must be obvious.

Willingly identify yourself with that which you most desire, knowing that it will find expression through you. Yield to the feeling of the wish fulfilled and be consumed as its victim, then rise as the prophet of the law of assumption.

CHAPTER XVII ALL THINGS ARE POSSIBLE

It is of great significance that the truth of the principles outlined in this book have been proven time and again by the personal experiences of the Author. Throughout the past twenty-five years he has applied these principles and proved them successful in innumerable instances. He attributes to an unwavering assumption of his wish already being fulfilled every success that he has achieved. He was confident that by these fixed assumptions his desires were predestined to be fulfilled. Time and again he assumed the feeling of his wish fulfilled and continued in his assumption until that which he desired was completely realized.

Live your life in a sublime spirit of confidence and determination; disregard appearances, conditions, in fact all evidence of your senses that deny the fulfillment of your desire. Rest in the assumption that you are already what you want to be, for in that determined assumption you and your Infinite Being are merged in creative unity, and with your Infinite Being (God) all things are possible. God never fails.

For who can stay His hand or say unto Him, What doest thou?

Through the mastery of your assumptions you are in very truth enabled to master life. It is thus that the ladder of life is ascended: thus the ideal is realized. The clue to the real purpose of life is to surrender yourself to your ideal with such awareness of its reality that you begin to live the life of the ideal and no longer your own life as it was prior to this surrender.

He calleth things that are not seen as though they were, and the unseen becomes seen.

Each assumption has its corresponding world. If you are truly observant, you will notice the power of your assumptions to change circumstances which appear wholly immutable.

You, by your conscious assumptions, determine the nature of the world in which you live. Ignore the present state and assume the wish fulfilled.

Claim it; it will respond. The law of assumption is the means by which the fulfillment of your desires may be realized. Every moment of your life, consciously or unconsciously, you are assuming a feeling. You can no more avoid assuming a feeling than you can avoid eating and drinking. All you can do is control the nature of your assumptions.

Thus it is clearly seen that the control of your assumption is the key you now hold to an ever expanding, happier, more noble life.

CHAPTER XVIII BE YE DOERS

Be ye doers of the word and not hearers only, deceiving your own selves. For if any be a hearer of the word, and not a doer, he is like unto a man beholding his natural face in a glass and goeth his way, and straightway forgetteth what manner of man he was. But whoso looketh into the perfect law of liberty, and continue therein, he being not a forgetful hearer but a doer of the work, this man shall be blessed in his deed. James 1:22- 25.

The word in this quotation means idea, concept, or desire. You deceive yourself by "hearing only" when you expect your desire to be fulfilled through mere wishful thinking. Your desire is what you want to be, and looking at yourself "in a glass" is seeing yourself in imagination as that person. Forgetting "what manner of man" you are is failing to persist in your assumption. The "perfect law of liberty" is the law which makes possible liberation from limitation, that is, the law of assumption.

To continue in the perfect law of liberty is to persist in the assumption that your desire is already fulfilled. You are not a "forgetful hearer" when you keep the feeling of your wish fulfilled constantly alive in your consciousness. This makes you a "doer of the work," and you are blessed in your deed by the inevitable realization of your desire.

You must be doers of the law of assumption, for without application the most profound understanding will not produce any desired result.

Frequent reiteration and repetition of important basic truths runs through these pages. Where the law of assumption is concerned — the law that sets man free — this is a good thing. It should be made clear again and again even at the risk of repetition. The real truth-seeker will welcome this aid in concentrating his attention upon the law which sets him free.

The parable of the Master's condemnation of the servant who neglected to use the talent given him is clear and unmistakable. Having discovered within yourself the key to the Treasure House, you should be like the good servant who by wise use multiplied by many times the talents entrusted to him. The talent entrusted to you is the power to consciously determine your assumption. The talent not used, like the limb not exercised, withers and finally atrophies.

What you must strive after is being. In order to do it is necessary to be. The end of yearning is to be. Your concept of yourself can only be driven out of consciousness by another concept of yourself. By creating an ideal in your mind, you can identify yourself with it until you become one and the same with the ideal, thereby transforming yourself into it.

"The dynamic prevails over the static; the active over the passive. One who is a doer is magnetic and therefore infinitely more creative than any who merely hear. Be among the doers.

CHAPTER XIX ESSENTIALS

The essential points in the successful use of the law of assumption are these: First, and above all, yearning; longing; intense, burning desire.

With all your heart you must want to be different from what you are. Intense, burning desire [combined with intention to make good] is the mainspring of action, the beginning of all successful ventures. In every great passion [which achieves its objective] desire is concentrated [and intentioned. You must first desire and then intend to succeed].

As the hart panteth after the water brooks, so panteth my soul after Thee, O God.

Blessed are they that hunger and thirst after righteousness for they shall be filled.

Here the soul is interpreted as the sum total of all you believe, think, feel, and accept as true; in other words, your present level of awareness. God, I AM, is the power of awareness, the source and fulfilment of all desire [understood psychologically. I am an infinite series of levels of awareness and I am what I am in accordance with where I am in the series]. This quotation describes how your present level of awareness longs to transcend itself. Righteousness is the consciousness of already being what you want to be.

Second, cultivate physical immobility, a physical incapacity not unlike the state described by Keats in his "Ode to a Nightingale."

A drowsy numbness pains my senses, as though of hemlock I had drunk.

It is a state akin to sleep, but one in which you are still in control of the direction of attention. You must learn to induce this state at will, but experience has taught that it is more easily induced after a substantial meal, or when you wake in the morning feeling very loathe to arise. Then you are naturally disposed to enter this state. The value of physical immobility exposes itself in the accumulation of mental force which absolute stillness brings with it. It increases your power of concentration.

Be still and know that I am God.

In fact, the greater energies of the mind seldom break forth save when the body is stilled and the door of the senses closed to the objective world.

The third and last thing to do is *to experience in your imagination what you would experience in reality had you achieved your goal. [You must gain it in imagination first, for imagination is the very door to the reality of that which you seek. But use imagination masterfully and not as an on- looker thinking of the end, but as a partaker thinking from the end.]* Imagine that you possess a quality or something you desire which hitherto has not been yours. Surrender yourself completely to this feeling until your whole being is possessed by it. This state differs from reverie in this respect: it is the result of a controlled imagination and a steadied, concentrated attention, whereas reverie is the result of an uncontrolled imagination — usually just a daydream. In the controlled state, a minimum of effort suffices to keep your consciousness filled with the feeling of the wish fulfilled. The physical and mental immobility of this state is a powerful aid to voluntary attention and a major factor of minimum effort.

The application of these three points:

1. Desire
2. Physical immobility
3. The assumption of the wish already fulfilled

is the way to at-one-ment or union with your objective. *[The first point is thinking of the end, with intention to realize it. The third point is thinking from the end with the feeling of accomplishment. The secret of thinking from the end is to enjoy being it. The minute you make it pleasurable and imagine that you are it, you start thinking from the end.]*

One of the most prevalent misunderstandings is that this law works only for those having a devout or a religious objective. This is a fallacy.

It works just as impersonally as the law of electricity works. It can be used for greedy, selfish purposes as well as noble ones. But it should al- ways be borne in mind that ignoble thoughts and actions inevitably result in unhappy consequences.

CHAPTER XX
RIGHTEOUSNESS

In the preceding chapter righteousness was defined as the consciousness of already being what you want to be. This is the true psychological meaning and obviously does not refer to adherence to moral codes, civil law, or religious precepts. You cannot attach too much importance to being righteous. In fact, the entire Bible is permeated with admonition and exhortations on this subject.

Break off thy sins by righteousness. Dan. 4:27.

My righteousness I hold fast, and will not let it go: my heart shall not reproach me so long as I live. Job 27:6.

My righteousness shall answer for me in time to come. Genesis 30:33.

Very often the words sin and righteousness are used in the same quotation. This is a logical contrast of opposites and becomes enormously significant in the light of the psychological meaning of righteousness and the psychological meaning of sin. Sin means to miss the mark. Not to attain your desire, not to be the person you want to be, is sinning. Righteousness is the consciousness of already being what you want to be. It is a changeless educative law that effects must follow causes. Only by righteousness can you be saved from sinning.

There is a widespread misunderstanding as to what it means to be "saved from sin." The following example will suffice to demonstrate this misunderstanding and to establish the truth. A person living in abject poverty may believe that by means of some religious or philosophical activity he can be saved from sin" and his life improved as a result If however, he continues to live in the same state of poverty, it is obvious that what he believed was not the truth, and, in fact, he was not "saved " On the other hand, he can be saved by righteousness. The successful use of the law of assumption would have the inevitable result of an actual change in his life. He would no longer live in poverty. He would no longer miss the mark. He would be saved from sin.

Except your righteousness shall exceed the righteousness of the scribes and Pharisees, ye shall in no wise enter into the kingdom of heaven. Matt. 5:20.

Scribes and Pharisees means those who are influenced and governed by the outer appearances — the rules and customs of the society in which they live, the vain desire to be thought well of by other men. Unless this state of mind is exceeded, your life will be one of limitation — of failure to attain your desires — of missing the mark — of sin. This righteousness is exceeded by true righteousness, which is always the consciousness of already being that which you want to be.

One of the greatest pitfalls in attempting to use the law of assumption is focusing your attention on things, on a new home, a better job, a bigger bank balance. This is not the righteousness without which you "die in your sins." Righteousness is not the thing itself; it is the consciousness, the feeling of already being the person you want to be, of already having the thing you desire.

Seek ye first the kingdom of God, and his righteousness; and all these things shall be added unto you. Matthew 6:33.

The kingdom (entire creation) of God (your I AM) IS within you. Righteousness is the awareness that you already possess it all.

CHAPTER XXI FREE WILL

The question is often asked, "What should be done between the assumption of the wish fulfilled and its realization?" Nothing. It is a delusion that, other than assuming the feeling of the wish fulfilled, you can do anything to aid the realization of your desire. You think that you can do something, you want to do something; but actually you can do nothing. The illusion of the free will to do is but ignorance of the law of assumption upon which all action is based. Everything happens automatically. All that befalls you, all that is done by you — happens. Your assumptions, conscious or unconscious, direct all thought and action to their fulfillment. To understand the law of assumption, to be convinced of its truth, means getting rid of all the illusions about free will to act. Free will actually means freedom to select any idea you desire. By assuming the idea already to be a fact, it is converted into reality. Beyond that, free will ends and everything happens in harmony with the concept assumed.

I can of mine own self do nothing . . . because I seek not mine own will, but the will of the Father which hath sent me.

In this quotation the Father obviously refers to God. In an earlier chapter, God is defined as I AM. Since creation is finished, the Father is never in a position of saying "I will be." In other words, everything exists, and the infinite I AM consciousness can speak only in the present tense.

Not my will but thine be done.

"I will be" is a confession that "I am not" The Father's will is always "I AM." Until you realize that YOU are the Father (there is only one I AM and your infinite self is that I AM), your will is always "I will be."

In the law of assumption your consciousness of being is the Father's will. The mere wish without this consciousness is the "my will." This great quotation, so little understood, is a perfect statement of the law of assumption.

It is impossible to do anything. You must be in order to do.

If you had a different concept of yourself, everything would be different. You are what you are, so everything is as it is. The events which you observe are determined by the concept you have of yourself. If you change your concept of yourself, the events ahead of you in time are altered, but, thus altered, they form again a deterministic sequence starting from the moment of this changed concept. You are a being with powers of intervention, which enable you, by a change of consciousness, to alter the course of observed events — in fact, to change your future.

Deny the evidence of the senses, and assume the feeling of the wish fulfilled. Inasmuch as your assumption is creative and forms an atmosphere, your assumption, if it be a noble one, increases your assurance and helps you to reach a higher level of being. If, on the other hand, your assumption be an unlovely one, it hinders you and makes your downward way swifter. Just as the lovely assumptions create a harmonious atmosphere, so the hard and bitter feelings create a hard and bitter atmosphere.

Whatsoever things are pure, just, lovely, of good report, think on these things.

This means to make your assumptions the highest, noblest, happiest concepts. There is no better time to start than now. The present moment is always the most opportune in which to eliminate all unlovely assumptions and to concentrate only on the good. As well as yourself, claim for others their Divine inheritance. See only their good and the good in them. Stir the highest in others to confidence and self-assertion by your sincere as- sumption of their good, and you will be their prophet and their healer, for an inevitable fulfillment awaits all sustained assumptions.

You win by assumption what you can never win by force. An assumption is a certain motion of consciousness. This motion, like all motion, exercises an influence on the surrounding substance, causing it to take the shape of, echo, and reflect the assumption. A change of fortune is a new direction and outlook, merely a change in arrangement of the same mind substance — consciousness.

If you would change your life, you must begin at the very source with your own basic concept of self. Outer change, becoming part of organizations, political bodies, religious bodies, is not enough. The cause goes deeper. The essential change must take place in yourself, in your own concept of self. You must assume that you are what you want to be and continue therein, for the reality of your assumption has its being in complete independence of objective fact and will clothe itself in flesh if you persist in the feeling of the wish fulfilled. When you know that assumptions, if persisted in, harden into facts, then events which seem to the uninitiated mere accidents will be understood by you to be the logical and inevitable effects of your assumption.

The important thing to bear in mind is that you have *infinite free will in choosing your assumptions, but no power to determine conditions and events. You can create nothing, but your assumption determines what portion of creation you will experience.*

CHAPTER XXII PERSISTENCE

And He said unto them, Which of you shall have a friend, and shall go unto him at midnight, and say unto him, Friend, lend me three loaves; for a friend of mine in his journey is come to me, and I have nothing to set before him? And he from within shall answer and say. Trouble me not; the door is now shut, and my children are with me in bed; I cannot rise and give thee. I say unto you. Though he will not rise and give him, because he is his friend, yet because of his importunity he will rise and give him as many as he needeth. And I say unto you. Ask, and it shall be given you; seek, and ye shall find; knock, and it shall be opened unto you. Luke I I:5-9.

THERE ARE three principal characters in this X quotation; you and the two friends mentioned. The first friend is a desired state of consciousness. The second friend is a desire seeking: fulfillment. Three is the symbol of wholeness, completion. Loaves symbolize substance. The shut door symbolizes the senses which separate the seen from the unseen. Children in bed means ideas that are dormant. Inability to rise means a desired state of consciousness cannot rise to you, you must rise to It. Importunity means demanding persistency a kind of brazen impudence. Ask, seek, and knock mean assuming the consciousness of already having; what you desire.

Thus the scriptures tell you that you must persist in rising to (assuming) the consciousness of your wish already being fulfilled. The promise is definite that if you are shameless in your impudence in assuming that you already have that which your senses deny, it shall be given unto yon- your desire shall be attained.

The Bible teaches the necessity of persistence by the use of many stories. When Jacob sought a blessing from the Angel with whom he wrestled he said I will not let thee go, except thou bless me.

When the Shunammite sought the help of Elisha she said.

As the Lord liveth, and as thy soul liveth, I will not leave thee, and he arose and followed her.

The same idea is expressed in another passage:

And he spake a parable unto them that men ought always to pray, and not to faint; saying, There was in a city a judge, which feared not God, neither regarded man, and there was a widow in that city; and she came unto him, saying. Avenge me of mine adversary. And he would not for a while; but afterward he said within himself. Though I fear not God, nor regard man; yet because this widow troubleth me, I will avenge her, lest she weary me by her continual coming. Luke 18:1-5.

The basic truth underlying each of these stories is that desire springs from the awareness of ultimate attainment and that persistence in maintaining the consciousness of the desire already being fulfilled results in its fulfillment.

It is not enough to feel yourself into the state of the answered prayer; you must persist in that state. That is the reason for the injunction Man ought always to pray and not to faint.

Here, to pray means to give thanks for already having what you desire. Only persistency in the assumption of the wish fulfilled can cause those subtle changes in your mind which result in the desired change in your life. It matters not whether they be "Angels," "Elisha," or "reluctant judges"; all must respond in harmony with your persistent assumption. When it appears that people other than yourself in your world do not act toward you as you would like, it is not due to reluctance on their part but a lack of persistence in your assumption of your life already being as you want it to be. Your assumption, to be effective, cannot be a single isolated act; it must be a maintained attitude of the wish fulfilled. [And that maintained attitude that gets you there, so that you think from your wish fulfilled instead of thinking about your wish, is aided by assuming the feeling of the wish fulfilled frequently. It is the frequency, not the length of time, that makes it natural. That to which you constantly return constitutes your truest self. Frequent occupancy of the feeling of the wish fulfilled is the secret of success.]

CHAPTER XXIII CASE HISTORIES

It will be extremely helpful at this point to cite a number of specific examples of the successful application of this law. Actual case histories are given. In each of these, the problem is clearly defined and the way imagination was used to attain the required state of consciousness is fully described. In each of these instances, the author of this book was either personally concerned or was told the facts by the person involved.

Case Study I

This is a story with every detail of which I am personally familiar.

In the spring of 1943 a recently drafted soldier was stationed in a large army camp in Louisiana. He was intensely eager to get out of the army, but only in an entirely honorable way.

The only way he could do this was to apply for a discharge. The application then required the approval of his commanding officer to become effective. Based on army regulations, the decision of the commanding officer was final and could not be appealed. The soldier, following all the necessary procedure, applied for a discharge. Within four hours this application was returned — marked "disapproved." Convinced he could not appeal the decision to any higher authority, military or civilian, he turned within to his own consciousness, determined to rely on the law of assumption.

The soldier realized that his consciousness was the only reality, that his particular state of consciousness determined the events he would encounter.

That night, in the interval between getting into bed and falling asleep, he concentrated on consciously using the law of assumption. In imagination he felt himself to be in his own apartment in New York City. He visualized his apartment, that is, in his mind's eye he actually saw his own apartment, mentally picturing each one of the familiar rooms with all the furnishings vividly real.

With this picture clearly visualized, and lying flat on his back, he completely relaxed physically. In this way he induced a state bordering on sleep, at the same time retaining control of the direction of his attention. When his body was completely immobilized, he assumed that he was in his own room and felt himself to be lying in his own bed-a very different feeling from that of lying on an army cot. In imagination he rose from the bed, walked from room to room touching various pieces of furniture. He then went to the window and with his hands resting on the sill looked out on the street on which his apartment faced. So vivid was all this in his imagination that he saw in detail the pavement, the railings, the trees and the familiar red brick of the building on the opposite side of the street. He then returned to his bed and felt himself drifting off to sleep. He knew that it was most important in the successful use of this law that at the actual point of falling asleep his consciousness be filled with the assumption that he was already what he wanted to be. All that he did in imagination was based on the assumption that he was no longer in the army. Night after night the soldier enacted this drama. Night after night in imagination he felt himself, honorably discharged, back in his home seeing all the familiar surroundings and falling asleep in his own bed. This continued for eight nights. For eight days his objective experience continued to be directly opposite to his subjective experience in consciousness each night, before going to sleep. On the ninth day orders came through from Battalion headquarters for the soldier to fill out a new application for his discharge. Shortly after this was done he was ordered to report to the Colonel's office. During the discussion the Colonel asked him if he was still desirous of getting out of the army. Upon receiving an affirmative reply, the Colonel said that he personally disagreed, and while he had strong objections to approving of the discharge, he had decided to overlook these objections and to approve it. Within a few hours the application was approved and the soldier, now a civilian, was on a train bound for home.

Case Study 2

This is a striking story of an extremely successful businessman demonstrating the power of imagination and the law of assumption. I know this family intimately, and all the details were told to me by the son described herein.

The story begins when he was twenty years old. He was next to the oldest in a large family of nine brothers and one sister. The father was one of the partners in a small merchandising business. In his eighteenth year the brother referred to in this story left the country in which they lived and traveled two thousand miles to enter college and complete his education. Shortly after his first year in college he was called home because of a tragic event in connection with his father's business. Through the machinations of his associates, the father was not only forced out of his business, but was the object of false accusations impugning his character and integrity. At the same time he was deprived of his rightful share in the equity of the business. The result was he found himself largely discredited and almost penniless. It was under these circumstances that the son was called home from college.

He returned, his heart filled with one great resolution. He was determined that he would become outstandingly successful in business. The first thing he and his father did was to use the little money they had to start their own business. They rented a small store on a side street not far from the large business of which the father had been one of the principal owners.

There they started a business bent upon real service to the community. It was shortly thereafter that the son, with instinctive awareness that it was bound to work, deliberately used imagination to attain an almost fantastic objective.

Every day on the way to and from work he passed the building of his father's former business — the biggest business of its kind in the country. It was one of the largest buildings, with the most prominent location in the heart of the city. On the outside of the building was a huge sign on which the name of the firm was painted in large bold letters. Day after day as he passed by, a great dream took shape in the son's mind. He thought of how wonderful it would be if it was his family that had this great building -his family that owned and operated this great business.

One day as he stood gazing at the building, in his imagination he saw a completely different name on the huge sign across the entrance. Now the large letters spelled out his family name (in these case histories actual names are not used; for the sake of clarity in this story we will use hypothetical names and assume that the son's family name was Lordard). Where the sign read F. N. Moth & Co., in imagination he actually saw the name, letter by letter, J. N. Lordard & Sons. He remained looking at the sign with his eyes wide open, imagining that it read J. N. Lordard & Sons. Twice a day, week after week, month after month for two years he saw his family name over the front of that building. He was convinced that if he felt strongly enough that a thing was true, it was bound to be the case, and by seeing in imagination his family name on the sign-which implied that they owned the business -he became convinced that one day they would own it.

During this period he told only one person what he was doing. He confided in his mother, who with loving concern tried to discourage him in order to protect him from what might be a great disappointment. Despite this, he persisted day after day. Two years later the large company failed and the coveted building was up for sale. On the day of the sale he seemed no nearer ownership than he had been two years before when he began to apply the law of assumption. During this period they had worked hard, and their customers had implicit confidence in them. However, they had not earned anything like the amount of money required for the purchase of the property. Nor did they have any source from which they could borrow the necessary capital. Making even more remote their chance of getting it was the fact that this was regarded as the most desirable property in the city and a number of wealthy business people were prepared to buy it. On the actual day of the sale, to their complete surprise, a man, almost a total stranger, came into their shop and offered to buy the property for them. (Due to some unusual conditions involved in this transaction the son's family could not even make a bid for the property.) They thought the man was joking. However, this was not the case. The man explained that he had watched them for some time, admired their ability, believed in their integrity, and that supplying the capital for them to go into business on a large scale was an extremely sound investment for him. That very day the property was theirs. What the son had persisted in seeing in his imagination was now a reality. The hunch of the stranger was more than justified. Today this family owns not only the particular business referred to but owns many of the largest industries in the country in which they live.

The son, seeing his family name over the entrance of this great building, long before it was actually there, was using exactly the technique that produces results. By assuming the feeling that he already had what he desired— by making this a vivid reality in his imagination— by determined persistence, regardless of appearance or circumstance— he inevitably caused his dream to become a reality.

Case Study 3

This is the story of a very unexpected result of an interview with a lady who came to consult me.

One afternoon a young grandmother, a business woman in New York, came to see me. She brought along her nine-year-old grandson, who was visiting her from his home in Pennsylvania. In response to her questions, I explained the law of assumption, describing in detail the procedure to be followed in attaining an objective. The boy sat quietly, apparently absorbed in a small toy truck while I explained to the grandmother the method of assuming the state of consciousness that would be hers were her desire already fulfilled. I told her the story of the soldier in camp who each night fell asleep, imagining himself to be in his own bed in his own home.

When the boy and his grandmother were leaving, he looked up at me with great excitement and said, "I know what I want and, now, I know how to get it." Surprised, I asked him what it was he wanted; he told me he had his heart set on a puppy. To this the grandmother vigorously protested, telling the boy that it had been made clear repeatedly that he could not have a dog under any circumstances . . . that his father and mother would not allow it, that the boy was too young to care for it properly, and furthermore the father had a deep dislike for dogs — he actually hated to have one around.

All these were arguments the boy, passionately desirous of having a dog, refused to understand. "Now I know what to do," he said. "Every night just as I am going off to sleep I am going to pretend that I have a dog and we are going for a walk." "No," said the grandmother, "that is not what Mr. Neville means. This was not meant for you. You cannot have a dog."

Approximately six weeks later, the grandmother told me what was to her an astonishing story. The boy's desire to own a dog was so intense that he had absorbed all that I had told his grandmother of how to attain one's desire — and he believed implicitly that at last he knew how to get a dog.

Putting this belief into practice, for many nights the boy imagined a dog was lying in his bed beside him. In imagination he petted the dog actually feeling its fur. Things like playing with the dog and taking it for a walk filled his mind.

Within a few weeks it happened. A newspaper in the city in which the boy lived organized a special program in connection with Kindness to Animals Week. All schoolchildren were requested to write an essay on "Why I Would Like to Own a Dog." After entries from all the schools were submitted and judged, the winner of the contest was announced. The very same boy who weeks before in my apartment in New York had told me "Now I know how to get a dog" was the winner. In an elaborate ceremony, which was publicized with stories and pictures in the newspaper, the boy was awarded a beautiful collie puppy.

In relating this story, the grandmother told me that if the boy had been given the money with which to buy a dog, the parents would have refused to do so and would have used it to buy a bond for the boy or put it in the savings bank for him. Furthermore, if someone had made the boy a gift of a dog, they would have refused it or given it away. But the dramatic manner in which they boy got the dog, the way he won the city- wide contest, the stories and pictures in the newspaper, the pride of achievement and joy of the boy himself all combined to bring about a change of heart in the parents, and they found themselves doing that which they never conceived possible — they allowed him to keep the dog.

All this the grandmother explained to me, and she concluded by saying that there was one particular kind of dog on which the boy had set his heart. It was a collie.

Case Study 4

This was told by the aunt in the story to the entire audience at the conclusion of one of my lectures.

During the question period following my lecture on the law of assumption, a lady who had attended many lectures and had had personal consulta-tion with me on a number of occasions rose and asked permission to tell a story illustrating how she had successfully used the law.

She said that upon returning home from the lecture the week before, she had found her niece distressed and terribly upset. The husband of the niece, who was an officer in the Army Air Force stationed in Atlantic City, had just been ordered, along with the rest of his unit, to active duty in Europe. She tearfully told her aunt that the reason she was upset was that she had been hoping her husband would be assigned to Florida as an Instructor. They both loved Florida and were anxious to be stationed there and not to be separated. Upon hearing this story, the aunt stated that there was only one thing to do and that was to apply immediately the law of assumption. "Let's actualize it," she said. "If you were actually in Florida, what would you do? You would feel the warm breeze. You would smell the salt air. You would feel your toes sinking down into the sand. Well, let's do all that right now."

They took off their shoes and turning out the lights, in imagination they felt themselves actually in Florida feeling the warm breeze, smelling the sea air, pushing their toes into the sand.

Forty-eight hours later the husband received a change of orders. His new instructions were to report immediately to Florida as an Air Force Instructor. Five days later his wife was on a train to join him. While the aunt, in order to help her niece to attain her desire, joined in with the niece in assuming the state of consciousness required, she did not go to Florida. That was not her desire. On the other hand, that was the intense longing of the niece.

Case Study 5

This case is especially interesting because of the short interval of time between the application of this law of assumption and its visible manifestation.

A very prominent woman came to me in deep concern. She maintained a lovely city apartment and a large country home; but because the many demands made upon her were greater than her modest income, it was absolutely essential that she rent her apartment if she and her family were to spend the summer at their country home.

In previous years the apartment had been rented without difficulty early in the spring, but the day she came to me the rental season for summer sublets was over. The apartment had been in the hands of the best real estate agents for months, but no one had been interested even in coming to see it.

When she had described her predicament I explained how the law of assumption could be brought to bear on solving her problem. I suggested that by imagining the apartment had been rented by a person desiring immediate occupancy and by assuming that this was the case, her apartment actually would be rented. In order to create the necessary feeling of naturalness - the feeling that it was already a fact that her apartment was rented - I suggested that she drift off into sleep that very night, imagining herself, not in her apartment, but in whatever place she would sleep were the apartment suddenly rented. She quickly grasped the idea and said that in such a situation she would sleep in her country home even though it was not yet opened for the summer.

This interview took place on Thursday. At nine o'clock the following Saturday morning she phoned me from her home in the country — excited and happy. She told me that on Thursday night she had fallen asleep actually imagining and feeling that she was sleeping in her other bed in her country home many miles away from the city apartment she was occupying. On Friday, the very next day, a highly desirable tenant, one who met all her requirements as a responsible person, not only rented the apartment, but rented it on the condition that he could move in that very day.

Case Study 6

Only the most complete and intense use of the law of assumption could have produced such results in this extreme situation.

Four years ago a friend of our family asked that I talk with his twenty-eight-year-old son who was not expected to live.

He was suffering from a rare heart disease. This disease resulted in a disintegration of the organ. Long and costly medical care had been of no avail. Doctors held out no hope for recovery. For a long time the son had been confined to his bed. His body had shrunk to almost a skeleton, and he could talk and breathe only with great difficulty. His wife and two small children were home when I called, and his wife was present throughout our discussion.

I started by telling him that there was only one solution to any problem, and that solution was a change of attitude. Since talking exhausted him, I asked him to nod in agreement if he understood clearly what I said. This he agreed to do. I described the facts underlying the law of consciousness — in fact that consciousness was the only reality. I told him that the way to change any condition was to change his state of consciousness concerning it. As a specific aid in helping him to assume the feeling of already being well, I suggested that in imagination, he see the doctor's face expressing incredulous amazement in finding him recovered, contrary to all reason, from the last stages of an incurable disease, that he see him double checking in his examination and hear him saying over and over, "It's a miracle—it's a miracle." He not only understood all this clearly, but he believed it implicitly. He promised that he would faithfully follow this procedure. His wife, who had been listening intently, assured me that she, too, would diligently use the law of assumption and her imagination in the same way as her husband. The following day I sailed for New York — all this taking place during a winter vacation in the tropics. Several months later I received a letter saying the son had made a miraculous recovery. On my next visit I met him in person. He was in perfect health, actively engaged in business and thoroughly enjoying the many social activities of his friends and family.

He told me that from the day I left he never had any doubt that "it" would work. He described how he had faithfully followed the suggestion I had made to him and day after day had lived completely in the assumption of already being well and strong.

Now, four years after his recovery, he is convinced that the only reason he is here today is due to his successful use of the law of assumption.

Case Study 7

This story illustrates the successful use of the law by a New York business executive.

In the fall of 1950 an executive of one of New York's prominent banks discussed with me a serious problem with which he was confronted. He told me that the outlook for his personal progress and advancement was very dim. Having reached middle age and feeling that a marked improvement in position and income was justified, he had "talked it out" with his superiors. They frankly told him that any major improvement was impossible and intimated that if he was dissatisfied, he could seek another job. This, of course, only increased his uneasiness. In our talk he explained that he had no great desire for really big money but that he had to have a substantial income in order to maintain his home comfortably and to provide for the education of his children in good preparatory schools and colleges. This he found impossible on his present income. The refusal of the bank to assure him of any advancement in the near future resulted in a feeling of discontent and an intense desire to secure a better position with considerably more money. He confided in me that the kind of job he would like better than anything in the world was one in which he managed the investment funds of a large institution such as a foundation or great university.

In explaining the law of assumption, I stated that his present situation was only a manifestation of his concept of himself and declared that if he wanted to change the circumstances in which he found himself, he could do so by changing his concept of himself. In order to bring about this change of consciousness, and thereby a change in his situation, I asked him to follow this procedure every night just before he fell asleep: In imagination he was to feel he was retiring at the end of one of the most important and successful days of his life. He was to imagine that he had actually closed a deal that very day to join the kind of organization he yearned to be with and in exactly the capacity he wanted. I suggested to him that if he succeeded in completely filling his mind with this feeling, he would experience a definite sense of relief. In this mood his uneasiness and discontent would be a thing of the past. He would feel the contentment that comes with the fulfillment of desire. I wound up by assuring him that if he did this faithfully, he would inevitably get the kind of position he wanted.

This was the first week of December. Night after night without exception he followed this procedure. Early in February a director of one of the wealthiest foundations in the world asked this executive if he would be interested in joining the foundation in an executive capacity handling investments. After some brief discussion he accepted.

Today, at a substantially higher income and with the assurance of steady progress, this man is in a position far exceeding all that he had hoped for.

Case Study 8

The man and wife in this story have attended my lectures for a number of years. It is an interesting illustration of the conscious use of this law by two people concentrating on the same objective at one time.

This man and wife were an exceptionally devoted couple. Their life was completely happy and entirely free from any problems or frustrations.

For some time they had planned to move into a larger apartment. The more they thought about it, the more they realized that what they had their hearts set on was a beautiful penthouse. In discussing it together, the husband explained that he wanted one with a huge window looking out on a magnificent view. The wife said she would like to have one side of the walls mirrored from top to bottom. They both wanted to have a wood-burning fireplace. It was a "must" that the apartment be in New York City.

For months they had searched for just such an apartment in vain. In fact, the situation in the city was such that the securing of any kind of apartment was almost an impossibility. They were so scarce that not only were there waiting lists for them, but all sorts of special deals including premiums, the buying of furniture, etc., were involved. New apartments were being leased long before they were completed, many being rented from the blueprints of the building.

Early in the spring after months of fruitless seeking, they finally located one which they seriously considered. It was a penthouse apartment in a building just being completed on upper Fifth Avenue facing Central Park. It had one serious drawback. Being a new building, it was not subject to rent control, and the couple felt the yearly rental was exorbitant. In fact, it was several thousand dollars a year more than they had considered paying. During the spring months of March and April they continued looking at various penthouses throughout the city but they always came back to this one. Finally they decided to increase the amount they would pay substantially and made a proposition which the agent for the building agreed to forward to the owners for consideration.

It was at this point, without discussing it with each other, each determined to apply the law of assumption. It was not until later that each learned what the other had done. Night after night, they both fell asleep in imagination in the apartment they were considering. The husband, lying with his eyes closed, would imagine that his bedroom windows were overlooking the park. He would imagine going to the window the first thing in the morning and enjoying the view. He felt himself sitting on the terrace overlooking the park, having cocktails with his wife and friends, all thoroughly enjoying it. He filled his mind with actually feeling himself in the penthouse and on the terrace. During all this time, unknown to him, his wife was doing the same thing.

Several weeks went by without any decision on the part of the owners, but they continued to imagine as they fell asleep each night that they were actually sleeping in the penthouse.

One day, to their complete surprise, one of the employees in the apartment building in which they lived told them that the penthouse there was vacant. They were astonished because theirs was one of the most desirable buildings in the city with a perfect location right on Central Park. They knew there was a long waiting list of people trying to get an apartment in their building. The fact that a penthouse had unexpectedly become available was kept quiet by the management because they were not in a position to consider any applicants for it. Upon learning that it was vacant, this couple immediately made a request that it be rented to them, only to be told that this was impossible. The fact was that not only were there several people on a waiting list for a penthouse in the building but it was actually promised to one family. Despite this the couple had a series of meetings with the management, at the conclusion of which the apartment was theirs.

The building being subject to rent control, their rental was just about what they had planned to pay when they first started looking for a pent- house. The location, the apartment itself, and the large terrace surrounding it on the South, West, and North was beyond all their expectations — and in the living room on one side is a giant window 15 feet by 8 feet with a magnificent view of Central Park; one wall is mirrored from floor to ceiling, and there is a wood-burning fireplace.

CHAPTER XXIV FAILURE

This book would not be complete without some discussion of failure in the attempted use of the law of assumption. It is entirely possible that you either have had or will have a number of failures in this respect - many of them in really important matters. If, having read this book, having a thorough knowledge of the application and working of the law of assumption, you faithfully apply it in an effort to attain some intense desire and fail, what is the reason? If to the question "Did you persist enough?" you can answer Yes - and still the attainment of your desire was not realized, what is the reason for failure?

The answer to this is the most important factor in the successful use of the law of assumption. The time it takes your assumption to become fact, your desire to be fulfilled, is directly proportionate to the naturalness of your feeling of already being what you want to be - of already having what you desire. The fact that it does not feel natural to you to be what you imagine yourself to be is the secret of your failure. Regardless of your desire, regardless of how faithfully and intelligently you follow the law, if you do not feel natural about what you want to be, you will not be it. If it does not feel natural to you to get a better job, you will not get a better job. The whole principle is vividly expressed by the Bible phrase "you die in your sins" — you do not transcend from your present level to the state desired.

How can this feeling of naturalness be achieved? The secret lies in one word — imagination. For example, this is a very simple illustration: Assume that you are securely chained to a large heavy iron bench. You could not possibly run, in fact you could not even walk. In these circumstances it would not be natural for you to run. You could not even *feel* that it was natural for you to run. But you could easily imagine yourself running. In that instant, while your consciousness is filled with your imagined running, you have forgotten that you are bound. In imagination your running was completely natural.

The essential feeling of naturalness can be achieved by persistently filling your consciousness with imagination- imagining yourself being what you want to be or having what you desire.

Progress can spring only from your imagination, from your desire to transcend your present level. What you truly and literally must feel is that with your imagination, all things are possible. You must realize that changes are not caused by caprice, but by a change of consciousness. You may fail to achieve or sustain the particular state of consciousness necessary to produce the effect you desire. But, once you know that consciousness is the only reality and is the sole creator of your particular world and have burnt this truth into your whole being, then you know that success or failure is entirely in your own hands. Whether or not you are disciplined enough to sustain the required state of consciousness in specific instances has no bearing on the truth of the law itself— that an assumption, if persisted in, will harden into fact. The certainty of the truth of this law must remain despite great disappointment and tragedy — even when you "see the light of life go out and all the world go on as though it were still day." You must not believe that because your assumption failed to materialize, the truth that assumptions do materialize is a lie. If your assumptions are not fulfilled, it is because of some error or weakness in your consciousness. However, these errors and weaknesses can be overcome. Therefore, press on to the attainment of ever higher levels by feeling that you already are the person you want to be. And remember that the time it takes your assumption to become reality is proportionate to the naturalness of being it. Man surrounds himself with the true image of himself. Every spirit builds itself a house and beyond its house a world, and beyond its world a heaven. Know then that the world exists for you. For you the phenomenon is perfect.

What we are, that only can we see. All that Adam had, all that Caesar could, you have and can do. Adam called his house, heaven and earth.

Caesar called his house, Rome; you perhaps call yours a cobbler's trade; a hundred acres of land, or a scholar's garret. Yet line for line and point for point, your dominion is as great as theirs, though without fine name. Build therefore your own world. As fast as you conform your life to the pure idea in your mind, that will unfold its great proportion.

Emerson

CHAPTER XXV FAITH

A miracle is the name given, by those who have no faith, to the works of faith.

Faith is the substance of things hoped for, the evidence of things not seen. Heb. 11:1.

The very reason for the law of assumption is contained in this quotation. If there were not a deep-seated awareness that that which you hope for had substance and was possible of attainment, it would be impossible to assume the consciousness of being or having it. It is the fact that creation is finished and everything exists that stirs you to hope — and hope, in turn, implies expectation, and without expectation of success it would be impossible to use consciously the law of assumption. "Evidence" is a sign of actuality. Thus, this quotation means that faith is the awareness of the reality of that which you assume, [a conviction of the reality of things which you do not see, the mental perception of the reality of the invisible]. Consequently, it is obvious that a lack of faith means disbelief in the existence of that which you desire. Inasmuch as that which you ex- perience is the faithful reproduction of your state of consciousness, lack of faith will mean perpetual failure in any conscious use of the law of assumption.

In all the ages of history, faith has played a major role. It permeates all the great religions of the world, it is woven all through mythology, and yet today it is almost universally misunderstood.

Contrary to popular opinion, the efficacy of faith is not due to the work of any outside agency. It is from first to last an activity of your own consciousness.

The Bible is full of many statements about faith, of the true meaning of which few are aware. Here are some typical examples:

Unto us was the gospel preached, as well as unto them: but the word preached did not profit them, not being mixed with faith in them that heard it. Heb. 4:2.

In this quotation the "us" and "them" make clear that all of us hear the gospel. "Gospel" means good news. Very obviously good news for you would be that you had attained your desire. This is always being "preached" to you by your infinite self. To hear that which you desire does exist and you need only to accept it in consciousness is good news. Not "mixing with faith" means to deny the reality of that which you desire. Hence there is no "profit" (attainment) possible.

O faithless and perverse generation, how long shall I be with you? Matt. 17:17.

The meaning of "faithless" has been made clear. "Perverse" means turned the wrong way, in other words, the consciousness of not being what you want to be. To be faithless, that is, to disbelieve in the reality of that which you assume, is to be perverse. "How long shall I be with you" means that the fulfillment of your desire is predicated upon your change to the right state of consciousness. It is just as though that which you desire is telling you that it will not be yours until you turn from being faithless and perverse to righteousness. As already stated, righteousness is the consciousness of already being what you want to be.

By faith he forsook Egypt, not fearing the wrath of the king: for he endured, as seeing him who is invisible. Heb. 11:27.

"Egypt" means darkness, belief in many gods (causes). The "king" symbolizes the power of outside conditions or circumstances. "He" is your concept of yourself as already being what you want to be. "Enduring as seeing him who is invisible" means persisting in the assumption that your desire is already fulfilled. Thus this quotation means that by persisting in the assumption that you already are the person you want to be, you rise above all doubt, fear, and belief in the power of outside conditions or circumstances; and your world inevitably conforms to your assumption.

The dictionary definitions of faith:

"the ascent of the mind or understanding to the truth" — "unwavering adherence to principle"

are so pertinent that they might well have been written with the law of assumption in mind. Faith does not question - Faith knows.

CHAPTER XXVI DESTINY

Your destiny is that which you must inevitably experience. Really it is an infinite number of individual destinies, each of which when attained is the starting place for a new destiny.

Since life is infinite, the concept of an ultimate destiny is inconceivable. When we understand that consciousness is the only reality, we know that it is the only creator. This means that your consciousness is the creator of your destiny. The fact is, you are creating your destiny every moment, whether you know it or not. Much that is good and even wonderful has come into your life without your having any inkling that you were the creator of it. However, the understanding of the causes of your experience, and the knowledge that you are the sole creator of the contents of your life, both good and bad, not only make you a much keener observer of all phenomena, but through the awareness of the power of your own consciousness, intensify your appreciation of the richness and grandeur of life.

Regardless of occasional experiences to the contrary, it is your destiny to rise to higher and higher states of consciousness, and to bring into manifestation more and more of creation's infinite wonders. Actually, you are destined to reach the point where you realize that through your own desire you can consciously create your successive destinies.

The study of this book, with its detailed exposition of consciousness and the operation of the law of assumption, is the master key to the conscious attainment of your highest destiny.

This very day start your new life. Approach every experience in a new frame of mind — with a new state of consciousness. Assume the noblest and the best for yourself in every respect and continue therein.

Make believe — great wonders are possible.

CHAPTER XXVII REVERENCE

Never wouldst Thou have made anything if Thou hadst not loved it. Wisdom 11:24.

IN ALL creation, in all eternity, in all the realms of your infinite being the most wonderful fact is that which is stressed in the first chapter of this book. You are God. You are the "I am that I am." You are consciousness. You are the creator. This is the mystery, this is the great secret known by the seers, prophets, and mystics throughout the ages. This is the truth that you can never know intellectually. Who is this you? That it is you, John Jones or Mary Smith, is absurd. It is the consciousness which knows that you are John Jones or Mary Smith. It is your greater self, your deeper self, your infinite being. Call it what you will. The important thing is that it is within you, it is you, it is your world. It is this fact that underlies the immutable law of assumption. It is upon this fact that your very existence is built. It is this fact that is the foundation of every chapter of this book. No, you cannot know this intellectually, you cannot debate it, you cannot substantiate it. You can only feel it. You can only be aware of it.

Becoming aware of it, one great emotion permeates your being. You live with a perpetual feeling of reverence. The knowledge that your creator is the very self of yourself and never would have made you had he not loved you must fill your heart with devotion, yes, with adoration. One knowing glimpse of the world about you at any single instant of time is sufficient to fill you with profound awe and a feeling of worship.

It is when your feeling of reverence is most intense that you are closest to God, and when you are closest to God, your life is richest.

Our deepest feelings are precisely those we are least able to express, and even in the act of adoration, silence is our highest praise.

www.ingramcontent.com/pod-product-compliance
Lightning Source LLC
Chambersburg PA
CBHW050023170726
48282CB00025B/524
* 9 7 8 8 1 1 9 2 1 4 1 2 9 *